VIRAL MYSTIFICATION

IMPACT OF SOCIAL MEDIA MARKETING ON THE HOSPITALITY INDUSTRY

ARSHAQ HABIB

XpressPublishing

An imprint of Notion Press

XpressPublishing
An imprint of Notion Press

Old No. 38, New No. 6
McNichols Road, Chetpet
Chennai - 600 031

ISBN 978-1-64899-548-4

Firstly I would like to thank my parents and family members for all the support. I am grateful to Dr. Wajeeda Bano, Economics Department and Dr. A M Khan for the encouragement. In particular I would like to thank my PhD supervisor Dr. Mustiary Begum at Mangalore University, Dr. Joseph PD, Coordinator of MBA (Tourism and Travel Management) Mangalore University, Prof Shekar Naik, Associate Professor of MBA (Tourism and Travel Management), Dr Jagath Thimmaiah, Principal of FMKMC college, Prof Shailashree K, Coordinator of Tourism and travel management for all the support. I would like to thank my best friend Prof. Noushad H, Assistant Professor at Government First Grade College Mudigere. I wish to place my gratitude to my colleagues and students of Field Marshal KM Cariappa College who has contributed directly or indirectly in the making of this book. Sincere thanks to my sister Fathima Afreen for editing and correcting this book. I would also like to thank Shameer SR for the guidance and the designing of this book.

Contents

Preface

The Internet has brought about a lot of changes in hotel industry, specifically on the marketing section. It has assisted the firms to collaborate and coordinate different activities and also reach the customers in different corners of the globe. Social media marketing is an important part of internet that helps the firm to stay connected to the customers. It comprises of aspects such as online advertising; publishing of credible information for customers; communicating with the customers through discussion forums, blogs, social networks and much more. Thus, social media marketing has a great deal of impact on the hotel industry itself. It helps to increase the customer base of the hotels by understanding their concerns, responding to their queries and also providing better services based on the opinions shared. Being an avid traveller myself, there have been instances wherein I have experienced manipulations through social media. However, considering my educational background and my work experience, I was eager to learn more about the social media marketing and its impact on hospitality industry. My experiences with tourism and its influence on internet in transforming the tourism industry is what influenced me to write this book.

CHAPTER ONE

INTRODUCTION

Prior to the emergence of Internet era, word-of-mouth was the main medium through which the customers would express their opinion regarding the products and services with their peers. But the current trend has transformed word of mouth to word of mouse and the customers are expressing their opinion regarding the products via social networking sites. This has led to the companies to involve social media into their marketing plan in order to stay in touch with their customers so that they can interact with them, know their views, solve their queries and stay ahead of their competitors. Internet has drastically changed the way in which marketing is done by the companies; it has persuaded the companies to enhance their interactivity, efficiency and innovativeness . The online platform provides an opportunity to the customers to share the information with a lot of people at once. This has led to the creation of awareness among the companies to communicate and interact with customers so that they can keep up a positive impression among the customers.Hotel industry is one of the booming industries in the world. With the raising competition, it has become important that the hotels retain their customers and also enhance their customer base. Social media marketing is the best tool to keep in touch with the customers and keep them happy, by addressing their queries and sorting out their problems.The author has chosen hotel Lotus Vacations for the purpose of this research. The reason for choosing Lotus Vacations hotel was that, this hotel has a tremendous mark in social media by its effective social media marketing. Selecting this hotel as case study for research helped the researcher in getting reliable and proficient information for the research.

Majority of the time spent by the internet users online is spent on social networking sites. The customers share their views regarding the products and services on their profile or the pages of the companies or groups etc. If the view of customers are positive, then this information shared by the customers act as free promotion for the company whereas if the review is bad, then this information acts as negative publicity which causes harm to the reputation of firms.This has made it important for the hotels to include social media marketing as a part of their marketing strategy. The main reason behind choosing this topic for research was that, the researcher felt that through this research, the hotels could understand the importance of social media marketing and also comprehend how they could implement it efficiently.Social media marketing is all about building relationships between the customer and the organisation by regular interaction online to communicate and share information on current trends. The higher degree of attachment associated with social networking platforms will induce loyalty according to him.

Right from the point of developing the product to its introduction and sustenance in the market to the process of improving customer's experience and everything encompasses is called Marketing. Customers' requirements and expectations must be at the core of the marketing strategy while devising the products and services of the hotels. Traditional knowledge exhorted marketing strategists to attract new customers to the hotels. This was given more importance than to keep the present customer base intact. The more recent views on marketing, though, lay equal importance to both aspects. It believes that negative publicity of unsatisfied ex-customers will hamper new prospects. Keeping with this view, hotels are now turning to social media marketing using internet to balance aforementioned requirements.

Social Media

Social media or network as an online platform where people with similar interests come and share ideas and communicate. As a virtual space to share experience and information, social media has penetrated all walks of the society and has transformed our very perspectives. The existence of a plethora of social media websites today and the ones which can actually propel marketing for hotel services have been listed and defined below:

1.
   Blogs: *Blogs are websites comprising generally of personal journals posted online, at times with hyperlinks and comments from the author. Various attributes of blogs like subscription, blog rolls, comments etc can be utilised to good effect by marketing agencies.*

2.
   Social Networks: *Social networks are web-based platforms wherein a user can create a public profile to interact with online and offline friends to share views and information. Some well known examples of social networking sites are given below:*

Facebook: *An average of 250,000 people log in to Facebook every day. One of the most popular social networking sites in the world, Facebook lets its users share pictures, videos and exchange information and communicate.*

Twitter: *Twitter is a microblogging site which allows users to update and read statuses, called tweets. An average of 3 million tweets are posted per day. Businesses can use this platform to strengthen relations with partners and future clients. Activities like sales, CRM, brand* *awareness etc is also aided.*

3.

Media Sharing: *These are websites which allow users to create, upload, view and share multimedia content online. Being very cheap, this provides as an efficient means for businesses to propagate their campaigns here effectively to millions of people. Some popular media sharing websites are:*

YouTube: *This is a video streaming website that allows users to view and upload videos. It's a free service with over 4 million monthly visitors (YouTube, 2014).*

Flickr: *Flickr is an online platform to upload, view and share photos and simultaneously interact with friends and others. People use Flickr mostly as a database to store and manage photos for personal blogs and websites.*

4.

Wikis: *These are websites that provide open ended documents online that can be edited by users. These provide information on various topics in multiple languages, like a giant online encyclopaedia. Users can modify existing documents. Wikipedia is a quintessential example.*

5.

Online Communities: *Online community is a virtual space where a group of individuals assemble to share thoughts, views and experiences. It may be a private or public community wherein members may put up threads of topics on which other members may comment. The community is kept active by such rituals.*

Online travel community is a vertical in this segment wherein people with specific interests in travel and tourism share their travel experiences, norms and values. With relation to hospitality industry, online communities are used by members to share their experience at a particular hotel and rate the services provided online so that other members may gain from collective experience and opinion.

Foursquare: *A popular online travel community is Foursquare, which allows people to share locations of their favourite places in the vicinity. Opinions and critiques are also shared helping customers choose wisely. It has a symbiotic model of working wherein customers are enticed to visit a place listed on foursquare often and the businesses that list themselves on this app can gain access to customer analytics to tailor the services to meet the requirements of the customers.*

6.

Forums and Reviewing Sites: *Websites that offer a platform for sharing reviews of the particulars in a specific sector are aplenty on the internet. With respect to the hotel industry such forums and reviewing sites helps travellers to document their past experiences at specific hotels regarding the quality of services and accommodation, thereby helping prospective clients make decisions. These platforms help competitors and the organisations themselves can get a wider perspective of the business from the eyes of the customers.*

7.

Discussion Forums: *As the name suggests, these are online platforms where users create profiles and engage in discussions with other users on a common topic. There would be different topics being simultaneously discussed in the forum moderated by administrators of the site. These discussions may be about reviews of products and services.*

Booking.com: *This is an accommodation booking website and a discussion forum. Previous customers can rate their experiences in various hotels and services provided by them and put up comments regarding the same. New customers can refer to these and make informed choices while selecting accommodation, which can be reserved simultaneously. Booking.com is available in 40 languages in over 180 countries worldwide.*

TripAdvisor.com: *TripAdvisor.com is an online tour guide and review sites. Around 90% of all tourists search online for reviews and recommendations regarding destinations and accommodations therein before making a trip.*

CHAPTER TWO

Implementation of Social Media Marketing and its impact

Setting Targets in Mass Public for Social Media Marketing

Like in every operation, in social media marketing too, the first step is to identify the target audience. This is followed by charting a course of action to go about the marketing and subsequent communications to the specified audience. This process of setting specific targets and strategizing real marketing steps not only helps the firm to achieve the goals but also to understand their utility. By postulating that the goals identified must me realistic, quantifiable, assessable and achievable within a specific time frame to ensure effective and desired outcome.

Generally the course of the marketing communication is determined by keeping the financial constraints as a benchmark and target completion rate is analysed at the end to know the level of success. Marketing communication as an effective tool is often neglected and this leads to marketing failures more often than not.The most widely used benchmark for devising a communication path is the proposed budget, unless there are other strategising goals involved.

The crux of the model or that of social media marketing, in general, is that the discourse with the public should not be discontinued under any circumstances, even if those circumstances propagate negative publicity for the firm. An article on Small Business (2014) argues that even in such cases, the conversation must be allowed to take its course as the social media is built upon a platform of collaborative interactions. If we observe the general occurrences in social media marketing worldwide, we find multiple instances wherein firms encounter negative publicity and criticism online. Unfortunately, it has been seen that several firms deal with this situation in an unprofessional manner. Some try to choke the conversation or halt it completely by finding those responsible for such material online and put constraints on them. Some others decide to be mute spectators and let the game play itself. Neither is advised. Muzzling the opinions of those who criticised the brand and asking them to undo their doing online will do more bad than good for the brand image and will hamper the growth of the firm. This might, in fact, be more damaging than being a silent spectator.The argument presented by Small Business (2014) and propose that the firms, in such trying conditions, must come out with dignified, calculated and modest statements to counter the criticisms. This actually helps to augment the goodwill for the brand among the onlookers as the brand would have managed a tortuous situation with tact. While making such statements, the organisation must try to incorporate the perspective of those who initiated such disparagement in the first place while ensuring that it doesn't lose the customers' loyalty because of this. Also, it is highly advised to use the local tongue while issuing such reactions. The whole purpose of such a statement must be to purge any negative opinions and to propagate the progress that the firm has made in spite of all the negative happenings.

Customer Reaction and Services

Online marketing, as a process, must focus on its specified target concerned with the browser location, network and kind of requests. Social media has revolutionised customer relation management and services in multiple ways. To begin with, the business used to reply to queries of clients online in a public manner so that others with similar concerns may view it. Later, this evolved to let the clients answer each others queries, thus taking the form of a mutually agreeable discussion. This allows the firm to manage multiple clients simultaneously in a cost effective manner. Though, there may be instances, wherein clients wish to keep their identities or concerns private and in such cases, the firms must provide solutions directly. It is best to not indulge middlemen for addressing the issues as the customers would be expecting a direct answer from an authentic source. All these aspects will have a positive impact on the company by improving their credibility and goodwill.

Credibility, Interaction and Participation

The aim of social marketing must be to provide genuine information to the customers regarding the details of the product being marketed. This is important as customers will not appreciate false propaganda. The author supports this postulate and further opines that social media marketing must be based on mutual trust and bonding. This can be augmented by efficient networking and constant conservations. The hotels must ensure that they respond to the concerns and grievances of the clients immediately.

Content Creation

The fact that the customers' reactions are at the centre of social media marketing makes it imperative that the information being promulgated by the hotels are genuine, eye-catching and impressive. Unabashed freedom given to the consumers will ensure that they despise futile information. The hotels take into account user sensibilities and the hotels' products and integrate them to create content on the internet to encourage and entice customers to visit their hotels.

Online Visibility and Data Supervision

All businesses have their own websites and profiles on social networking sites to ensure pervasive online presence. This not only helps them to market their products and services efficiently but also helps gauge positioning in the market by analysing search engine results. The most beneficial aspect concerning social media marketing is that it allows supervision and analysis of all the data being used in the internet for marketing. The customers' feedback and other details help them to alleviate defects in the existing strategies. The fact that a prospective clientele can be surmised from analysing those who visit the profiles and websites of firms. This analysis helps to understand the interests and concerns of the customers and their feedback and suggestions and also the count and behaviour of customers who are regulars and those otherwise. From these numbers the relative popularity of the firm may be ascertained. There have been several tools that have been developed to help the firms attain these objectives in a more efficient manner. Some such tools are Google AdWord and Google Analytics. Google AdWord helps to improve online visibility simultaneously with search engine marketing (AdWord Official, 2014). Google Analytics is another useful tool which helps keep track of the customers' interests based on their arrival and departure (Google Analytics Official, 2014).

Overall Impact of Social Media Marketing on hotel industry

The existing marketing strategies of the hotel and the proposed social media marketing strategy must be completely complementary. Integrating the social media into their marketing procedures is imperative, which requires proper planning and strategising. Videos, photos and allied information regarding the hotel must be posted online on blogs and social media sites to ensure maximum visibility and augment online positioning. As a cheap tool to enhance the hotel's brand value, social media marketing must be utilised efficiently to reap maximum benefits. If the hotels serve their customers well, these satisfied customers are most likely to share their wonderful experience on their profiles online. This will encourage other prospective clients to approach the same hotel, courtesy the good opinion being floated about it. It is, therefore, obvious that the social media helps hotels build a customer base. The reverse possibility is equally probable. If the hotels provide unsatisfactory services, the customers will make their disapproval public online and this negative publicity will erode customer loyalty further and will cause a depletion of the customer base.As has been discussed earlier in this section, the world is on a fast track towards a virtual world. Hotel industries forecast a vital transition in the marketing aspects which is being promoted by social media marketing. The author advise the hotels to divert funds from conventional marketing methods into social media marketing to enhance productivity.

CHAPTER THREE

Methodology

Introduction

Research methodology entails the core of the research work which determines the type of work that has been put into the project. The course of action undertaken by the researcher to meet the objectives of the research and accomplish the aims therein is called the Research methodology, which constitutes various elements like the various philosophies subscribed to, the kind of approach undertaken, the methods used and the sources of data used and how they were assimilated in the first place inter alia. This chapter seeks to shed light on the kind of methodology adopted by this author to give effect to this research work and also justifies the choices that had been made in the process.

Research Philosophy

Research philosophy decides the behaviour of the research and has a direct bearing on the results therein. The course through which data is collected and the way in which it is modified and interpreted to arrive at a conclusion depends on the underlying philosophy employed by the researcher in the process. Conventionally, three types of philosophies exist viz. Positivism, Realism and Interpretivism. Positivism is the approach wherein rational and scientific inferences are drawn from the analysis of the research data. Realism puts more emphasis on the perspective of the researcher and his/her personal perceptions and understanding of the subject are used to realistically evaluate the data collected in the process of the research. It is an approach centred around individuals. Interpretivism is a broader perspective which accounts for the opinions of the various individuals and groups who are directly or indirectly a part of the research . Based on these interactions, more authentic inferences may be made by the researcher.

Choice of Research Philosophy and Justification

This author has chosen Realism as the preferred philosophy for this work. The research work intends to analyse the impact of social media in marketing in the hospitality industry and thus, requires analysis of several dependent and independent variables. Also, emphasis needs to be given to the understanding that the researcher has about the subject. Also, real world implications may be concentrated upon. Considering that no new theories are to be developed from this research, realism is the most suitable philosophy for the given scenario.

Research Approach

Research approach concerns with how the aims will be met and what direction the procedures will take. The various strategies pertaining to it constitute the approach. Broadly speaking, there are two varieties of research approaches viz. the Inductive approach and the Deductive approach.

Inductive approach involves formulating concepts and theories based upon hypotheses which are supplemented with data which are collected through the course of the research. The deductive approach on the other hand is the mirror opposite wherein the hypothesis is made first. This is followed by collection of data, which on analysis will corroborate the preconceived notions. Based upon this, the validity of the hypothesis may be ascertained.

Justification of Chosen Research Approach

The researcher has decided to use a deductive approach in this research. With an initial hypothesis that social media marketing is complementing marketing in hospitality industry, the data is collected, collated and analysed to prove whether this hypothesis is true or false. Comparison of various dependent and independent variables is also possible in this approach which allows for attaining a more credible and accurate result.

Research Design

One of the most important aspects of a research is the method of research chosen to arrive at a sensible result towards the end. The research method or design as it is sometimes called, decides the quality and constitution of the results obtained from a research. Depending upon the requirements of a research work, the researcher invariably chooses between two commonly used research methods or an amalgam of them viz. Qualitative and quantitative method.

Qualitative Method

Qualitative method has its base in intensive data collection through narrative. It's a subjective, holistic and process-oriented approach. The sampling will be specific with a small sample space intended to generate a thorough understanding of the matter under contention. The dependence on literature will be minimal. The data is collected in the forms of emotions and opinions of the people, which will be analysed later from which tentative conclusions will be drawn by the researcher.

Qualitative Method

Qualitative method is a generally deductive approach which is based on outcomes and is objective in nature. The data collection is in the form of statistics. Extensive review of associated literature is involved here to frame the relevant questionnaires. The sampling is random and will involve a large sample space. The data collected will be in the form of numbers and frequencies of various responses, thereby helping generate a trend in opinions of the respondents from which valuable generalisations may be made.

Justification for Chosen Research Design

The author, here, has chosen a mix of both the qualitative and quantitative methods. The specific requirements of the research work were considered to arrive at this decision. The objective of the research is to understand the impact of social media, a relatively new technology, in the marketing sphere of the hotel industry. This would require data from all levels of the hierarchy. The qualitative method will help get opinions and perspectives of the managers, which would help the author understand how the firm is affected by the social media marketing. The quantitative method involves a survey of the employees which helps to arrive at a generalized view of how the employees see this change. A combination of both these methods will help in better coverage of the topic and will also provide a self-correcting mechanism.

Data Collection Methods

Data is indispensable, no matter what the research concerns. The method employed to collect the data plays an indomitable role in determining the credibility and the efficacy of the results of the research work. Broadly, there are two types of data which are to be collected viz. the primary data and the secondary data. The primary data is the one which is collected in situ i.e. on the field with direct interactions with participants in the form of personal interviews, surveys or discussions with focus groups et al. It is done with specific impetus on the research being pursued. The secondary data, on the other hand, is basically accruing data present in existing works of previous researchers on similar topics. Authentic textbooks, educational websites, online journals, magazines, periodicals etc may be resorted to avail the said information. This is used to understand the topic in detail and formulate a theoretical framework for the furtherance of the research work.

Justification of the Data Collection Method Chosen

The researcher had chosen a combination of primary and secondary data for this research as theoretical base was required for this novel topic as well as a practical overview of the current scenario was required to completely account for the impact of social media marketing on the hotel industry.

Method of Primary Data Collection

The primary data was collected using both qualitative and quantitative approaches. Two managers were interviewed from the firm under consideration, as a part of the qualitative approach. They were chosen from those willing to take part in the study. The interview was held at their office, according to their convenience. A total of 8 questions were asked and the responses were documented. Supplementary questions were included to clarify any doubts. The questions are included in the Appendix. Interview was chosen by the researcher as it would provide clearer and credible primary data to the researcher. Under the quantitative approach, 50 employees from the organisation were selected at random and were provided with a previously prepared questionnaire, which they were asked to fill out. This was done online for logistical convenience. The questionnaire consisted of some general queries regarding demographic details and the rest concerning directed queries about the matter of contention. It was ensured that the questionnaire was first tested by the author for any discrepancies by subjecting it to a pilot run among some colleagues. This approach of subjecting a large sample space to a survey is cost effective and helps in generalisation at a larger scale with a fair degree of accuracy. The data so collected was later analysed and inferences were drawn.

Method of Secondary Data Collection

The secondary data was collected by careful perusal of authentic textbooks by yesteryear researchers about social media marketing. Online resources were depended upon to a fair degree. Literature on hospitality industry, tourism, social media and marketing were analysed. Online databases of EBSCO Host, Google Scholar and Science Direct were used. International journals like International Journal of Hospitality Management, Journal of Hospitality and Tourism Research et al and similar magazines were also referred. The data regarding Internet and the growth and subsequent boom of the social media were collected. Traditional marketing methods and how they are giving way to the more modern methods were also studied. The data which was collected was analysed by categorising them under certain parameters like study design, empirical or conceptual research, sample size, response rate, main analysis inter alia. The secondary data was used to create a framework based on which primary data collection was done. The analysis of this data formed the basis of the research.

Sampling Technique

Sampling process involves selecting a small subset from a large sample space. This process may be done in two manners. Either the sample may be selected at random, wherein everyone has an equal chance of being selected and there will be no prejudices involved. This is called Probability Sampling. Another manner is called Non-Probability Sampling wherein a particular sample set is chosen based on some preconceived criteria to suit a particular requirement.

Justification of Sampling Technique Chosen

Non-probability sampling, to be specific, Judgemental sampling is utilized to choose the respondents for interview. Judgemental sampling was chosen because this kind of sampling had put the author in a position where he can choose the right respondents who had sufficient knowledge about the subject matter of study. Whereas for Survey, Probability Sampling is chosen herein, as the requirement of the research is the understanding of the impact of social media on the employees, in terms of marketing sphere. To generate a fair opinion of the organisation, randomisation of opinions is of utmost importance. For the quantitative analysis the author sent 60 questionnaires to randomly selected employees via mail and of the responses 50 were chosen, again at random for further analysis.

Ethical Considerations

Ethical considerations are of prime importance when the research deals with such a vast repository of personal data of people subjected to the research. It reflects the personal integrity of the author and will also have a palpable bearing on the research. The UK Data Protection Act, 1998 defines the procedures that are to be followed by organisations and individuals in possession of personal data, in a manner that is not detrimental to anyone.

In pursuance of this, the author has ensured that the consent of all those being a part of the research was received beforehand. To this effect, a consent letter was prepared and attached to the questionnaire which was circulated among the potential respondents. The purposive sample of managers was also made aware of their rights to withdraw at any point of time from the participation. This clause was included in the survey questionnaire too. The participants were assured that the data being collected therein would only be used for purely academic purposes and would be subject to utmost confidentiality.

CHAPTER FOUR

DATA PRESENTATION, EVIDENCE, ANALYSIS AND DISCUSSION

The data pertaining to the impact of social media marketing in the hospitality industry, with special impetus of The Lotus Vacations has been assimilated and analysed herewith. The primary data has been considered in this section. The author has chosen to resort to a careful mix of both qualitative and quantitative approaches to collect this data. The qualitative analyses included personal interview of two managers in The Lotus Vacations. The interview was intended to gain insights into their predispositions regarding the impact and value of social media marketing in the realm of the hotel industry. A total of 8 questions were asked to this effect. So as to consolidate the information gathered by this means, the author chose to reinforce it with data collected by quantitative approach. Here, 50 employees of The Lotus Vacations were subjected to a survey. Questions were designed to generate demographic details as well as the personal opinions of the employees regarding the impact of social media marketing. Prepared questionnaires were supplied to them and their responses were collected and collated for further analyses. A careful mix of qualitative and quantitative approach was chosen so as to know the individual opinions at the higher level of the hierarchy as well as to see whether it is in sync with the general opinion further lower in the corporate structure.

Qualitative Analysis

The qualitative analysis involved personal interview of two managers of the hotel, to whom 8 questions were asked. The responses to these questions are documented below separately and analysed to identify the patterns and strategies employed by the hotel in the field of social media marketing.

1.

What do you think has been the impact of internet on the hotel marketing industry?

Respondent 1

"One simply cannot overemphasise the impact that the Internet has had in our daily lives. The hotel industry is no exception. It has led to diversification of products, automation and integration of multiple chains of services among other things. It has revolutionised the way we see the business."

Respondent 2

"There isn't a single sector of activity which hasn't experienced the effect of the phenomenon i.e. the Internet. It has helped us a great deal in our industry. Marketing, communication and integration of various activities pertaining to the institution are now much more effective and productive, thanks to the internet."

Source: Primary Data

Discussion: *Both the managers acknowledge the revolutionising impact that the internet has had in the hotel industry. Internet has enabled effective multilateral interactions plausible and helps industries manage their portfolios and services in a much more professional manner.*

2.
What is your view on social media marketing? What do you think is the role played by social media marketing in hotel industry?

Respondent 1:

Social media is an indispensable part of our marketing paraphernalia now. It helps us maintain constant communication with our clientele and prospective clients world over. Social media guarantees maximum visibility from a marketing perspective and helps share information and even opinions among ourselves and our customers.

Respondent 2

"Social media is the biggest tool that the internet has provided us with, with respect to marketing. Its omnipresence is a boon to our industry as it's the most cost effective means out there. It enables us to market our products and services efficiently and also helps us to

keep track about the present trends and the requirements of the customers.”

Source: Primary Data

Discussion:*Social media marketing is extremely important from a marketing perspective for the hotel industry. The relationship building between the customer and the organisation have been substantiated by both the managers.*

3.

According to you, what are the aspects that comprise the social media marketing?

Respondent 1

“Social media is a very broad term, which basically implies an online platform for exchange of information and opinions. Social networking sites like Facebook, LinkedIn and media sharing sites like YouTube are, in my opinion, the important ones in social media. Social media marketing comprises of advertising on media sharing and networking sites and garnering public opinion about them. Addressing a mass audience and encouraging consumer interaction in the social media platform is the main aspect of social media marketing.”

Respondent 2

“The main constituent is the large scale advertising of the product or service using photos, videos and other associated information. Credible exchange of opinions and information is another aspect. Participation of the clients must be voluntary and their opinions must be taken seriously. Brand value of the hotel can be improved incessantly using intelligent content creation and proper utilisation of available resources.”

Source: Primary Data

Discussion:*The two managers paint similar pictures regarding the various aspects of social media marketing. Their opinion can be generalised to depict that the main constituents of social media marketing are advertisements and other propaganda regarding their products. The upward scaling of the communication between clients and organisation has also been noticed. The credibility aspect, emphasised has also been included by the managers as an aspect of marketing via social media.*

4.

Has the Social Media Marketing increased competition in the hotel industry? If yes, why do you think it has increased competition? If no, why do you think it has failed to increase competition?

Respondent 1

"Yes, of course. The fact that a majority of the prospective clients and present customer base spend their time online these days makes it imperative that we use the social media to optimum effect. Almost every player in the segment has realised this and this has led to high competition in the field."

Respondent 2

"I do not believe that the competition has increased per say. For an established brand like ours, social media has just provided a new avenue for the manifestation of the existing competition in a fresh paradigm. Though, among emerging organisations the competition might have definitely increased because the immense potential of prospective clients leads to higher demand which creates an equivalent number of new suppliers."

Source: Primary Data

Discussion:*The managers provide a seemingly conflicted opinion upon this matter. The competition has definitely increased, at least, in some quarters with the high exposure that clients are receiving online. The choices available today are aplenty, which makes it imperative that the brands constantly improve upon their services so as to not be rendered archaic.*

5.

Has presence in Social Media brought in more customers to the Hotel? If yes, what according to you are the factors of social media marketing that increased the customers to the hotel? If no, why do you think it failed to attract more customers?

Respondent 1

"Yes, it has. Social media has helped us expand our client base and has allowed us to improve our service delivery and grievance redressal mechanisms. This has helped us to

maintain our traditional loyal customers as well as to attract new customers. Word of mouth is the best marketing that a firm can get and social media has revolutionised it to an extent, unforeseen hitherto."

Respondent 2

"Social media has helped us improve target marketing and has also helped us to understand the reactions of the customers to our services. It helps us devise customised strategies to enthuse target audience in an economically viable manner. Also, a very amicable relationship develops between the consumer and the organisation through constant communications. This has helped us augment our client base."

Source: Primary Data

Discussion: Both managers underscore the fact that social media marketing has improved their client base. They attribute this to improved market investigation and better consumer grievance redressal. Maintaining loyal customers while increasing new ones via positive reviews as one method how hotels increase their customers. This has been corroborated by the response of the managers.

6.
Have you faced any criticism/ negative feedback due to social media with respect to your business? If yes were you able to address it?

Respondent 1

"Catering to every individual's requirements is next to impossible. While designing our services, therefore, it is possible that certain customers feel that their interests have been compromised. It has happened on very few occasions and the customers have either used our feedback system, the online community of our hotel or the social networking page of our hotel to bring it to our notice. Our policy is to ensure that opinions of the customers are of utmost importance. We, therefore, take immense efforts to accommodate these interests."

Respondent 2

"Some customers have, at times, given some sort of negative feedback regarding some aspects of our services, using our online and offline mechanisms for the same. We have made it a point to encourage such feedbacks as it helps us serve our clients better and make

our brand better. We take immense efforts to rectify the issues pertaining to the feedbacks. Constant communications with the customers are maintained to encourage them to talk freely and share their thoughts and opinions."

Source: Primary Data

Discussion: Both the managers cite it as a company policy to encourage feedback, whether positive or negative, from the customers to help maintain an amicable relationship between them. The efficient management of customer reactions and subsequent services, are implemented by the hotel, according to their managers. They ensure the free flow of information and opinions through a credible medium to paint a winsome picture of their brand among the audience. Also, concerted efforts directed at remedying customer grievances are another step in the positive direction.

7.

Do you think social media will become business imperative for your hotel in the near future?

Respondent 1

"Yes, definitely. In a few short years, social media has become an indispensable part of our personal lives. Considering that and how the industries worldwide have incorporated the various tools that social media provides us to market our products and gauge its popularity, I think that in the near future this trend is only likely to grow further. The competition in the hotel industry is increasing and we have to constantly improve our standing by innovating in our services and accommodating our customers. Social media helps us achieve that in a cost-effective manner."

Respondent 2

"As most industries are starting to realise the potential of social media marketing, it is only natural that its role in future marketing endeavours will only expand. There are several ways to analyse customer requirements, their reactions and their preferences using social media with several tools that are available. With the striding developments in information technology that we are seeing today, these are only going to portend an upward trend. Further investment in this segment in the future is therefore inevitable."

Source: Primary Data

Discussion:The general perception of both managers suggests that the social media is here to stay and prosper. They intend to invest more in social media marketing to stay competitive in the hotel industry. This advocates incessantly to increase the proportion of investment into the burgeoning social media sector. The managers also believe higher degree of interaction with the customers in order to improve strategy building and service delivery.

8.

According to you, how can the companies make optimum utilization of their resources to improve on their social media marketing?

Respondent 1:

"Social media provides equal opportunity to all competitors in the field and how we utilise them will determine our success. For optimum utilisation, I believe customers must be given a free hand to voice their opinions and ideas regarding the services and products. Enough investment must be made to incorporate social media marketing paraphernalia into our present systems. The advertising done must be credible and concise, with proper market analysis and customer targeting. New tools available for the same must be employed."

Respondent 2:

"The potential of social media for marketing is immense. We want to maximise our visibility on the social platforms by flagging off energetic campaigns. The interaction and participation of the members of the online communities has to be encouraged to build loyalty. Content creation should be authentic. Also, it is imperative to have an offline conversion of the online impact that this would create, which can be ensured by altering our strategies to incorporate changing trends."

Source: Primary Data

Discussion: The managers further emphasise upon improving online visibility and encouraging customer interaction and participation. Use of new tools has also been cited by them, which probably includes those like Google AdWord and analytics as has been discussed before in this report. Efficient customer targeting is also considered . The organisation intends to invest more in the emerging social media marketing campaign to reap its rich dividends.

Quantitave Analysis

The quantitative approach included a survey of 50 employees of the hotel using previously prepared questionnaires. Their responses were collected, collated and assorted to give detailed data about their opinion regarding the various matters relating to the use of social media in the hotel's marketing. The information gathered has been documented in a tabulated and concise manner herewith, with some emphasis on some conspicuous points.

- *A careful blend of the young and the experienced can be seen in the workforce, as can be gauged from the nearly equitable distribution on the pie chart.*

- *A majority of the workforce falls within the 3-10 years range while those with above 10 years of experience are the least in number, among the respondents.*

- *Each one of the respondent strongly agrees with the fact that internet has made drastic changes in the hotel marketing industry. The unequivocal response to the query underlines the impact that the internet has had in the industry. Everyone, from the relatively fresh employees to the most experienced believes that internet has changed their industry. This finding supports the view of managers, that internet has truly brought about a lot of changes in hotel marketing industry.*

- *All the employees acknowledge that their firm employs social media marketing in their campaigns. As a continuance of the previous question, the employees present a uniform opinion here too, regarding the extent of penetration of social media in their marketing ventures. This is in line with the qualitative analysis carried out before.*

- *90% of the respondents are strongly in favour of social media marketing in the promotion of their hotels, while it is interesting to note that a 10% population, notably from the >10 years experience category seem a little apprehensive about the same. This could be attributed to the inertia hindering a transition from traditional methods to contemporary ones. The managers also had a similar view that social media marketing is an important tool for marketing and this view was also supported by various authors strongly favouring social media marketing.*

- *YouTube and the various news sites prove to be the most preferred sites for marketing by the respondents while Twitter, Facebook and LinkedIn come as second preferences. Also the conspicuous absence of support to Twitter and Facebook from the >5 years experience category shows that these websites are more suitable for a youth-oriented marketing only.*

- *As everyone had agreed to the impact of internet and the penetration of social media marketing into their industry, it is only natural that the respondents believe that this strategy would augment their revenue as well. Social media marketing can enrich the revenue generation of hotel by improving its brand image and customer loyalty.*

- *The interesting point to be noted here is that all the respondents with <5 years of experience, with one exception, chose cost reduction, better customer services and better reputation whereas everyone in the >5 year experience category chose competitive advantage and better customer relationship as the most important benefits. The findings gained from this query are in line with the opinion of various authors who also stated the above to be advantages of social media marketing.*

- *A majority of the respondents feel that their current strategy of social media marketing is either excellent or good. A miniscule 4%, notably from the >10years experience category, believe it is only satisfactory. This shows a trend as was noticeable from an earlier question too.*

- *The primary data has been collected and assimilated by means of qualitative and quantitative approach and it has been assorted and studied. The information gathered as a result has been documented and analyzed in this chapter. The researcher will utilize the analysis made to answer the research questions that is stated in the next chapter.*

CHAPTER FIVE

SUMMARY AND CONCLUSIONS

The final chapter of this research intends to consolidate the work that has been done hitherto. The author intends to draw inferences from the data collected and portray them in a concise manner. The manner in which the aims and objectives of the research were completed will also be discussed. Some recommendations on how to improve the application of social media marketing in the hotel industry will also be made. The research aim was to conduct an inquiry into the impact of the social media in the marketing paradigm in the hotel industry, with special reference to The Lotus Vacations. A theoretical framework for the same had to be first created using a secondary data collection and analysis followed by corroboration using primary data. The advantages of social media marketing and its potential had to be analysed. This has been successfully achieved in this research.

Answering the Research Questions

1.

What has been the impact of internet on the hotel marketing industry?

A: The Internet has left an indelible impression upon the hotel industry, especially in the marketing segment. This research work concentrates on a specific aspect of the internet viz. the social media and its impact on the hotel marketing industry. It has been substantially proven that the marketing has evolved from being just an exercise of advertising a product. With the advent of the internet, the marketing procedure has diversified, becoming a full fledged business in itself. It has helped integrate the various activities and coordinate them whilst they unfold at different corners of the world so as to provide a seamless and effective result. The competition also has multiplied manifold as a result of this. This has been inferred from the academic readings that had been done, which portrays the intense impact of internet in this industry. Moreover, this has been substantiated by both the qualitative and quantitative analysis, wherein both the managers as well as the employees acknowledged the effect that the internet has in the industry.

2.

What aspects comprise the social media marketing phenomena?

A: The secondary data collected from journals, academic books and other authentic sources have helped form an idea regarding the various aspects of social media marketing. Advertising using photos, videos, articles and other paraphernalia about the products and services on offer through the online platform is one of the main aspects. Ensuring maximum visibility of the product by encouraging constant communication and interaction among the participants in the online communities and discussion forums regarding the products and services is another constituent. Frank, uninhibited conversations must be allowed. The credibility, authenticity and utility of the matter being published are of utmost importance. The extent of freedom and anonymity that a random user gets in the virtual world must be taken into account while marketing online. Market analysis and collecting information from the usage trends and analysis of opinions generated is an indispensable facet. It helps in better audience targeting and also to devise customised strategies to enthuse specific clients. Social media marketing, being a relatively recent but extremely popular phenomenon has a repository of academic material on it which duly explains the various aspects. The managers of the hotel have also helped the author to verify these aspects in practical applications, with their answers to the queries.

3.

What role is the marketing via social media playing in the hospitality industry?

A: Social media is playing an extensive role in the marketing of the services of the hospitality industry. It has helped increase the number of customers according to the managers. The employees also feel that the role being played by social media in marketing is immense. The marketing now is a more intimate process, courtesy the social media. The interactions of the customers via the online platforms are the most important factor contributing to this aspect. As has been emphasised earlier, this type of marketing provides twin advantages of being able to judge the mindset of the customers at a given point of time as well as being able to provide them with the best of services based on their feedback and other opinions shared. The role played by marketing via social media is best explained by the response of the employees in the Lotus Vacations hotel. With a miniscule exception, all the respondents are very excited regarding the potential of the social media. The managers are also eager to etch out new plans to tap this resource further.

4.

What recommendations can be made for optimum utilisation of the resources available via the social media to prop up the marketing facet of the hotel industry?

A: The social media has revolutionised the way people communicate today and it has had its positive impact on the marketing industry as well. It is obvious that the marketing in the hospitality industry using the social media is a feature with immense potential and we are barely scratching the surface as of now. These have been developed by the author based on his findings from the secondary data being collected from academic woks and the on-field practical aspects which were made familiar, courtesy the primary data collected by the qualitative and quantitative approaches. Some recommendations to tap this resource have been enumerated below:

1.

Increase the amount of investment into the social media marketing wing to ensure maximum benefits from it. Development of newer technologies along the lines of Google analytics and AdWord must be pioneered, so as to increase the efficiency of marketing.

2.

Use various social media websites like Facebook and LinkedIn and the specialised tools that they provide to augment marketing. Further expand the reach by popularising the pages of the concerned organisations.

3.

Train the employees and others associated with the organisation to accustom them to enable them to effectively use the social media resource. This will help expanding the degree of visibility as more people will be helping to make the product better and more effective.

4.

Establish a special social media marketing sector within the company to exclusively manage it. This will improve efficiency and also enhance the cost benefit ratio.

5.

Importance must be given to ensure that the customer grievance redressal system linked to the social media marketing network is taken care of.

Practical Implications of this Research

This research work intends to have a robust application in both the academic segment as well as the industrial realm. The field of social media marketing, especially in the hospitality industry, being a novelty has immense and international scope for research. This work, building upon the credible work of stalwarts in the field, intends to be but a minor stepping stone to the researchers in the future in this subject.

The practical implications of this research arise from the fact that the world is living online today. Every activity is happening online today. It is imperative that the companies shift their focus from offline activities to online ones so as to gain maximum advantage of this rising tide in favour of the internet. Using the social media to great effect is an indispensable ingredient in the recipe for success in the coming days. In such a situation, this research intends to provide an insight into what social media marketing is all about and how it can be utilised efficiently to reap maximum benefits in marketing in a cost effective manner.

Research Limitations

The research had its limitations considering only two managers are being interviewed. Their views may or may not be representative. Also, the survey of 50 employees may not be enough to draw sweeping conclusions. But due to logistical considerations and time constraints, the research has to be limited in this manner. Nevertheless, Impetus was given on secondary data to offset these drawbacks. The convenience of the managers and the employees had to be sought before the interview, which was cumbersome, given their busy schedule. Nevertheless, proper planning of other facets of the research was done by the researcher to give enough buffer time for this part of the research to take place uninterrupted.

Scope for further research

Further research can be conducted on the same topic by choosing a larger sampling size and also by specifically focusing on one or more social networking sites. The researcher has chosen interview for collecting qualitative data, but the researcher opines that focus groups can also be effective to derive a large amount of useful data. This research was conducted taking a five star hotel as case study; further study could also be conducted by taking economy hotels as case study in order to understand the impact of social media marketing on economy hotels.

Conclusion

The final chapter in this research work was intended to consolidate the findings of the research and present them in a concise manner. The qualitative and quantitative data were analysed in the previous chapters and drawing from them the inferences were made in this chapter. This was used to answer the research questions as well. The various recommendations on how to improve upon and extract the maximum potential out of the resource that is social media marketing in the hospitality industry has also been included in this chapter. The practical and academic relevance of the research has also been explained.

References

AdWords Official, 2014, "How It Works", http://www.google.com/adwords/how-it-works/ads-on-google.htmlAccessed on 27th May 2014

Agresta, S. Bough, B, B. and Miletsky, J, I. (2010), "Perspectives on Social Media Marketing", Cengage Learning PTR.

Barker, M., Barker, D, I. and Bormann, N, F. (2012), "Social Media Marketing: A Strategic Approach", Cengage Learning.

Bryman, A. (2010), "Social Research Methods", 3rd Edition, Oxford, Oxford University Press.

Carboni, C. (2013), "Social Media Marketing: Hotel Industry Edition", Create The Dream.

Chaffey, D. and Bosomworth, D. (2012), "Creating a Social Media Marketing Strategy: Need to Know Guide", http://www.carmichaelcentre.ie/sites/default/files/Need-to-know-social-media-strategy-smart-insights_0.pdfAccessed on 26th May, 2014.

Clough, P. and Nutbrown, C. (2012), "A Student's Guide to Methodology", SAGE.

Creswell, J. (2009), "Research design qualitative, quantitative and mixed methods approaches", Sage Publications.

Crowther, D. and Lancaster, G. (2012), "Research methods", Routledge publishers.

Dawson, C. (2009), "Introduction to Research Methods: A Practical guide for any undertaking research project", 4th Edition, Sage Publication

Fuchs, C. (2013), "Social Media: A Critical Introduction", SAGE Publications.

Goddard, W. (2008), "Research Methodology: An introduction", New age international publisher.

Google Analytics Official, (2014),"Features", http://www.google.co.in/analytics/features/Accessed on 28th May, 2014.

Greenhalgh, N. (2014), "Hotels: Best Social Media Practices", MTG Media Group.

Gunelius, S. (2010), "30-Minute Social Media Marketing: Step-by-step Techniques to Spread the Word About Your Business", McGraw Hill Professional.

Jackson, S, L. (2008), "Research methods: a modular approach", Thomson Wadsworth Publication

Kang, J. (2011), "Social Media Marketing in the Hospitality Industry", Iowa State University.

Kerpen, D. (2011)," Likeable Social Media: How to Delight Your Customers, Create an Irresistible Brand, and Be Generally Amazing of Facebook", McGraw-Hill.

Kinsy, J. (2011), "Advertising and Social Media", ABA Bank Marketing.

Kumar, R. (2010), "Research Methodology: A Step-by-Step Guide for Beginners", Sage publications.

Langmia, K., Tyree, T., O'Brien, P. and Sturgis, I. (2013), "Social Media: Pedagogy and Practice", University Press of America.

Lohr, S, L. (2009), "Sampling: design and analysis", Brooks/Cole Publications

Mandiberg, M. (2012), "The Social Media Reader", NYU Press.

Martins, E. (2014), "Social Media Marketing: Secrets to Success", CreateSpace Independent Publishing Platform.

Mashable, (2014), "How Social Media is Changing Paid, Earned and Owned Media", http://mashable.com/2011/06/23/paid-earned-owned-media/accessed on 26th May, 2014.

Mennen, M. (2010), "Applied Research Methods for Business and Management" GRIN Verlag publishers.

Lotus Vacationshotel, (2014), "About Us", http://www.Lotus_Vacationshotel.com/about-usAccessed on 20th June, 2014.

Mukherji, P. and Albon, D. (2009), "Research Methods in Early Childhood: An Introductory Guide", Sage Publications

Muller C., 2011, "The Impact of Internet and Social Media on Hotel Industry", GRIN Verlag.

Noor al-Deen, H, S. and Hendricks, J, A. (2011), "Social Media: Usage and Impact", Lexington Books.

Safko, L. (2012), "The Social Media Bible: Tactics, Tools, and Strategies for Business Success", Wiley.

Saunders, M., Mark, L., Lewis, C, J., Philip, M, K., Thornhill, D. and Adrian, L. (2007), "Research Methods for Business Students", 4th Edition, Pearson Education.

Saunders, M. et al, (2009), "Research Methods for Business Students", 3rd Edition Prentice Hall.

Schaefer, M, W. (2014), "Social Media Explained: Untangling the World's Most Misunderstood Business Trend", Mark W. Schaefer.

Scott, D, M. (2013), "The New Rules of Marketing and PR: How to Use Social Media, Online Video, Mobile Applications, blogs, News Releases, and Viral Marketing to Reach Buyers Directly", Wiley.

Shoemaker, S., Lewis, R, C. and Yesawich, P, C. (2006), "Marketing Leadership in Hospitality and Tourism", Prentice Hall.

Small Business, (2014), "Social Media and Hospitality Industry", http://smallbusiness.chron.com/social-media-hospitality-industry-37599.htmlAccessed on 26[th]May, 2014.

The Entrepreneur, (2014), "Social Media Marketing", http://www.entrepreneur.com/topic/social-media-marketingAccessed on 27[th]May, 2014.

Tutel, T, L. and Solomon, M, R. (2012), "Social Media Marketing", Prentice Hall.

Vogt, W, P., Vogt, E, R., Gardner, D, C. and Haeffele, L, M. (2014), "Selecting the Right Analyses for Your Data: Qualitative, Quantitative and Mixed Approaches", Guilford Publications.

Waad, A. and Gomez, J, M. (2013), "Social Network in Marketing: Opportunities and Risks", http://www.lib.umich.edu/articles/details/FETCH-proquest_dll_26651871011Accessed on 28[th]May, 2014.

Walker, S. (2014), "Social Media Marketing Tips: Essential Strategy Advice and tips for Business: Facebook, Twitter, Google+, YouTube, LinkedIn, Instagram and Much More!", CreateSpace Independent Publishing Platform.

YouTube, (2014), "About YouTube", http://www.youtube.com/yt/about/Accessed on 27[th]May, 2014,

Zarei, E. (2014), "Social Media Marketing", Lulu.com

www.ingramcontent.com/pod-product-compliance
Lightning Source LLC
Chambersburg PA
CBHW081324250726
48662CB00008B/2741